CONTENTS

S0-EDB-181

"QUOTATIONS

from

PRESIDENT RON"

compiled by

Morton & Margaret Mintz

Futura

A Futura Book

First published in Great Britain in 1986 by
Father/Daughter Ventures

This edition published in 1987 by
Futura Publications,
a Division of Macdonald & Co (Publishers) Ltd
London & Sydney

ISBN 0 7088 3637 2

Typeset by Leaper & Gard Ltd, Bristol, England
Printed and bound in Great Britain by
Cox & Wyman Ltd, Reading

Futura Publications
A Division of
Macdonald & Co (Publishers) Ltd
Greater London House
Hampstead Road
London NW1 7QX
A BPCC plc Company

—————————————— ★ ——————————————

"And I just learned from being rebutted a couple of times that I'd better be sure of my facts."[1]

"... and I would like to match my accuracy with that of the media and I think I'd come out on top."[2]

1. Presidential candidate Ronald Reagan, 3 April 1980.
2. President Ronald Reagan, 27 January 1982.

THE GERONTOLOGIST

"If I became president, other than perhaps Margaret Thatcher, I will probably be younger than almost all the heads of state I will have to do business with."

"Giscard d'Estaing of France is younger than you," said interviewer Tom Brokaw.

"Who?" said the presidential candidate.

"Giscard d'Estaing of France," Brokaw repeated.

"Yes, possibly," Reagan said. "Not an awful lot more."

■ Reagan, then being 68, was 15 years older than the French leader.
Not to mention 21 years older than Spain's Adolfo Suarez, 19 years older than Australia's Malcolm John Fraser, 9 years older than Mexico's Jose Lopez Portillo, 8 years older than Italy's Guilio Andreotti, 7 years older than West Germany's Helmut Schmidt and Egypt's Anwar Sadat, and 2 years older than Israel's Menachem Begin.

Interview on NBC's "Today" program, 13 November 1979.

THE HOST I & II

"Chairman Mo."

■ The title and name bestowed on the head of state of Liberia, Samuel K. Doe, by the President when he introduced his White House guest in the Rose Garden. By then, the titles Doe had given himself included: Master Sargeant Doe, General Doe, and Commander-in-Chief Dr. Doe.

"Hello, Mr Mayor."

■ At a reception for black mayors Reagan, mistaking his only black cabinet member, Samuel Pierce, for a mayor, greeted him thus.

---

1. 17 August 1982.
2. The Observer, 5 January 1986.

THE HOST III & IV

"We're proud to have Sugar Ray and Mrs. Ray here."

■ The President's welcome to boxer Sugar Ray Leonard and his wife when they visited the White House, home of Ronnie and Mrs. Ronnie, during "Sugar Ray Leonard Day."

"Nice to see you again Mr Ambassador."

■ The President's welcome to Denis Healey on his arrival at the Oval Office, much to the horror of Sir Anthony Acland, Britain's Ambassador in Washington.

---

1. 23 September 1981.
2. The Observer, 29 March 1987.

THE SHEEP IN WOLF'S CLOTHING

"We weren't out to kill anybody."

■　The President's response to a question about whether the United States was trying to kill the leader of Libya in the bombing raid on Tripoli. There were scores of casualties including an undetermined number of deaths. Children were among the innocent victims.

Reporters shouted the question as Reagan made his way to a helicopter on 18 April 1986, three days after he had ordered the raid.

On the same day, the most prominent headline in the Washington Post was: "Qaddafi Was/A Target/of U.S. Raid/'Hoped We'd Get Him,' Official Says;/1 Jet Aimed at Compound."

THE EYEBALLER

"They blinked."

■ Reagan's answer on being asked why the
Soviets had broken the month-long stalemate
in the negotiations over Nicholas S. Daniloff by
allowing the U.S. correspondent to depart
Moscow. He left it to Secretary of State George
P. Shultz to explain why, only 24 hours later,
the administration had allowed Gennardi F.
Zakharov, the Soviet employee of the United
Nations it had accused of spying, to make a
quick plea in court and depart New York.

Reagan and Shultz had refused repeatedly to
exchange a "spy" for "an innocent hostage."
Now, they denied that the Daniloff departure
and the Zakharov plea-and-flee resulted —
could *only* have resulted — from just such a
trade.

When asked later whether the Soviets had blinked, the
President replied:

"I shouldn't have said that. No comment."

Reagan made the claim while campaigning on 20 September
1986. He disclaimed it — i.e. blinked — on 30 September.

THE COUNTER-TERRORIST I

"Anyone that's ever had their kitchen done over knows that it never gets done as soon as you wish it would."

■ This remark to reporters followed the bombing of the incomplete U.S. Embassy in a Beirut suburb in which two Americans and at least ten Lebanese employees died.

23 September 1983

THE COUNTER-TERRORIST II

"I think that these terrorist attacks [in Lebanon] attest to the success we were having."

■ The President said this at a breakfast with reporters at the White House, four months after the truck bombing that killed 241 U.S. Marines at the Beirut airport on 23 October 1983.

---

15 February 1984.

THE FAITHFUL FRIEND

"Can we abandon this country [South Africa] that has stood beside us in every war we've ever fought?"

■ South Africa's ruling National Party and the Afrikaaner community tried but failed to keep their country out of World Wars I and II.

Mark Green, Newsday; 2 December 1981

THE ADMIRER

"They [South Africa] have eliminated the segregation that we once had in our own country — the type of thing where hotels and restaurants and places of entertainment and so forth were segregated — that has all been eliminated."

Phone interview with WSB Radio of Atlanta; broadcast 26 August 1985.

THE HEMISPHERIC
GEOGRAPHER I

"And now, would you join me in a toast to President Figueirdo, to the people of Bolivia — that's where I'm going — to the people of Brazil, and to the dream of democracy and peace here in the Western Hemisphere."

■   Where El Presidente was going, and did go, was Bogota, Colombia; where he was not going, and did not go, was Bolivia.

Toast at a dinner hosted by Brazilian President Figueiredo, Brasillia, 1 December 1982.

THE HEMISPHERIC
GEOGRAPHER II

"I didn't go down there with any plan for the Americas, or anything. I went down to find out from them and [learn] their views. You'd be surprised. They're all individual countries."

■   Said in reply to a reporter's question whether his trip to Latin America had changed his views about the region.

Washington Post, 6 December 1982.

THE EQUALIZER I

"They are the moral equivalent of our Founding Fathers."

■ Reagan was speaking about the contras, the U.S. backed rebels in Nicaragua.

Remarks at Conservative Political Action Conference, 1 March 1985.

THE EQUALIZER II

"I would say that the individuals that went there [to Spain] were, in the opinion of most Americans, fighting on the wrong side."

■ The President was drawing an analogy between the nearly 3,000 Americans who fought in the Abraham Lincoln Brigade in the Spanish Civil War of 1936-1939 and the Americans in Central America who were aiding the contras in Nicaragua a half-century later.

The Americans in Spain were volunteers defending a democratically-elected government ["the wrong side"] against military rebels whose allies, Hitler and Mussolini, provided bombers and divisions of troops. In fact, most Americans favored the Spanish government: 65 percent in 1937, 76 percent in 1938.

The Americans aiding the contras are mercenaries who operate from U.S.-subsidized sanctuaries against a U.S.-recognized foreign government. U.S. laws prohibit conspiracies to harm the property of, and the use of U.S. soil to launch a military expedition against, such a government.

Interview with Scripps-Howard editors and writers on 23 October 1984. On 8 October 1986, in talking to reporters, Reagan again used the Brigade as a precedent for "his miserable little war," as Ring Lardner, Jr. called it in the New York Times on 23 October 1986. Lardner had more reason than most to protest: his brother James was killed while fighting with the Brigade.

THE PAPAL NUNCIO

"I just had a verbal message delivered to me from Pope John Paul, urging us to continue our efforts in Central America."

■ The Pope at once denied that he had sent this message, which Reagan divined to be encouragement for his campaign for Capitol Hill support of the contras.

Conference on Religious Liberty; remarks to delegates, 16 April 1985.

THE BULL IN A CHINA SHOP

Reporter: "Are you still for 'official relations' with Taiwan, yes or no?"

Reagan: "Um, I guess it's a yes."

■ This exchange occurred at a press conference on 22 August 1980. Peking responded the next day with a charge that Reagan, in what was "absolutely not a slip of the tongue," had "insulted one billion Chinese people." Reagan then pulled back, stating on 25 August: "I don't know that I said that or not, ah, I really don't; I mis-stated."

All of the quotations appeared in the New York Times.

THE VIETNAM HISTORIAN I

"If I recall correctly, when France gave up Indochina as a colony, the leading nations of the world met in Geneva in regard to helping those colonies become independent nations. And since North and South Vietnam had been previous to colonization two separate countries, provisions were made that these two countries could by a vote of all their people together decide whether they wanted to be one country or not."

■ When France colonized Vietnam it was *one* country but was divided into three provinces. While France reunited the country (under Emperor Bao Dai), much of it remained loyal to Ho Chi Minh. The Geneva conference called for the north and south to be partitioned temporarily, until reunification elections would be held two years later, in 1956.

News Conference, 18 February 1982.

THE VIETNAM HISTORIAN II

"And there wasn't anything surreptitious about it, but when Ho Chi Minh refused to participate in such an election and there was provision that the peoples of both countries could cross the border and live in the other country if they wanted to, and when they began leaving by the thousands and thousands from North Vietnam to live in South Vietnam, Ho Chi Minh closed the border and again violated that part of the agreement."

■ After Emperor Bao Dai was deposed, it was Ngo Dinh Diem, president of *South* Vietnam, who refused to participate in the elections. Senior American officials, fearing that Ho Chi Minh would win and unify the country, favored delaying the elections, and in 1954, the CIA undertook a covert operation intended to destabilize Ho Chi Minh in the north.

News Conference, 18 February 1982.

THE VIETNAM HISTORIAN III

"And openly, our country sent military advisers there to help a country which had been a colony have such things as a national security force, an army if you might say, or a military, to defend itself. And they were doing this, I recall correctly, also in civilian clothes, no weapons, until they began being blown up where they lived, in walking down the street by people riding on bicycles and throwing pipe bombs at them, and then they were permitted to carry side arms or wear uniforms ..."

■ During the period under discussion — the early 1960s — U.S. military advisers, in uniform, trained South Vietnamese forces, and terrorist attacks against Americans had not yet become a serious problem.

News Conference, 18 February 1982.

THE VIETNAM HISTORIAN IV

"But it was totally a program until John F. Kennedy, when these attacks and forays became so great, that John F. Kennedy authorized the sending in of a division of Marines, and that was the first move toward combat moves in Vietnam ..."

■ President Kennedy did not dispatch Marine or other ground-combat units to South Vietnam. Rather, he authorized "combat support" of Vietnamese forces. The support was substantial, including armed helicopters, fighter aircraft, and, ultimately, 19,000 so-called advisers. The first Marine combat brigade went to Vietnam in 1965, under orders of President Johnson.

News Conference, 18 February 1982.

THE THEOLOGIAN I

"You might be interested to know that the Scriptures are on our side on this."

■ Reagan was enlisting the Bible, specifically, Luke 14:31, on behalf of his vast armaments program.

Meeting with a group of business and trade representatives, 4 February 1985.

THE THEOLOGIAN II

"Well, I don't think I've ever used the Bible to further political ends or not, but I've found that the Bible contains an answer to just about everything and every problem that confronts us, ..."

■ After being criticized for saying that Scripture sanctions the U.S. arms buildup, Reagan was asked if "you don't have any problem with using the Bible in a political context?"

News Conference, 21 February 1985.

THE BARRISTER

"In England, if a criminal carried a gun, even though he didn't use it, he was not tried for burglary or theft or whatever he was doing, he was tried for first-degree murder and hung if he was found guilty."

■ Reagan apparently referred to a law providing for the execution of a person convicted of having *used* a gun in committing a crime in which a person died, not for execution of a person who simply had carried a gun. Despite himself having been nearly killed by a would-be assassin who had easily obtained a pistol although deranged, Reagan has been steadfast in his opposition to strict gun-control legislation.

Question-and-answer session with students at St. Peter's Catholic Elementary School, Geneva, Illinois, 15 April 1982.

THE POLES VAULTER

"Arriving in Warsaw in 1977 President Carter got off the plane to announce to a startled satrap who rules the country on behalf of the Soviet Union, 'Our concept of human rights is preserved in Poland.'"

■   What Carter actually said was: "I think that our concept of human rights is preserved in Poland, as I've said, *much better than [in] some other Eastern European countries with which I'm familiar*."

  Haynes Johnson reported in the Washington Post that, as a presidential candidate, Reagan repeated his distorted charge "in every address" he made in the week ending 3 February 1980.

Washington Post, 4 February 1980.

THE DIETETIST

The Russians "cannot vastly increase their
military productivity because they've already
got their people on a starvation diet of
sawdust. ..."

Remarks at a meeting of reporters and editors, 18 January 1981.

THE SOVIET HISTORIAN

"Now, just the other day, one among you ... has quoted the Ten Commandments of Nikolai Lenin, that he'd printed as the ten principles — guiding principles of Communism."

■ If Lenin's given name was Nikolai, it's jolly Saint Vladimir Hyich who arrives each Christmas in the reindeer-drawn sled. Or, as some Soviets said, maybe they should be calling George Washington "Bill". Lenin, whether N. or V.I., never handed down "Ten Commandments" of Communism.

Press Conference, 20 January 1982.

THE WORD DROPPER

"I'm no linguist, but I have been told that in the Russian language there isn't even a word for freedom."

■   Freedom in Russian is *svoboda*.

BBC Interview, 29 October 1985.

THE PSYCHOTHERAPIST

"And I felt that since the German people — and very few alive that remember even the war, and certainly none of them who were adults, and participating in any way — and they have a feeling, and a guilt feeling that's been imposed upon them, and I just think it's unnecessary."

■ Reagan had been asked to say why his exclusion of a Nazi concentration camp site from his planned trip to Germany would fulfill his goal of "commemorating V-E Day." His suggestion that no living person who was an adult in World War II remembers it, is, of course, preposterous. There are millions of Germans who were, say; 18 to 21 on V-E Day in 1945, and who were only 58 to 61 when the 76-year-old President spoke.

News Conference, 21 March 1985.

THE VICTIMOLOGIST

"They were victims, just as surely as the victims in the concentration camps."

■ The President's explanation of his decision to lay a memorial wreath in a cemetery at Bitburg in which German soldiers are buried alongside Nazi SS troopers.

Session with Regional Editors and Broadcasters, 18 April 1985.

THE WAR VETERAN

"Yes, I know all the bad things that happened in that war. I was in uniform for four years myself."

■ The President was referring to Nazi war atrocities in World War II. His military service was in Hollywood — in the First Motion Picture Unit of the Army Air Corps at the old Hal Roach studios.

Interview with foreign journalists, 29 April 1985.

THE DESEGREGATIONIST

"... when the Japanese dropped the bomb on Pearl Harbor there was a Negro sailor whose total duties involved kitchen-type duties. ... He cradled a machine gun in his arms, which is not an easy thing to do, and stood on the end of a pier blazing away at Japanese airplanes that were coming down and strafing him, and [segregation] was all changed."

- This was Reagan's "cinematic version of how segregation had ended in the armed forces," Washington Post reporter Lou Cannon wrote in his biography; *Reagan.* But it was an executive order of President Truman that actually ended segregation in the armed forces, and he signed the order in 1948 — seven years after Pearl Harbor, and three years after World War II.

1975 campaign for the presidential nomination

THE SPORTS CHRONICLER

"At that time, the opening lines of the *Official Baseball Guide* read, 'Baseball is a game for Caucasian gentlemen.'"

■ Reply when asked in Charlotte, North Carolina, whether blacks in the South needed to demonstrate to get the right to vote. Reagan, once a radio sportscaster in Des Moines, Iowa, was claiming that baseball ceased being a whites-only game because he and other sportscasters editorialized against this racism.

"He makes no mention of Jackie Robinson, who broke the major leagues' color barrier fully 10 years after Reagan left Des Moine," Jules Witcover and Richard M. Cohen wrote. "As for the opening line in the *Baseball Guide*, in St. Louis, Editor Joe Marchin takes out one *Guide* from the 1930s, and then another, but he can't find that sentence. Finally, he says, 'That's bullshit.'"

Esquire, March 1976. Witcover and Cohen were Washington Post reporters.

THE ENFORCER

"I favor the Civil Rights Act of 1964 and it must be enforced at gunpoint if necessary."[1]

"I would have voted against the Civil Rights Act of 1964."[2]

---

1. 20 October 1965.
2. Quoted by Curt Gentry, *The Last Days of the Great State of California*.
   The contrasting quotations were cited by the Citizen Research Group in *Selecting a President; A Citizen Guide to the 1980 Election/A Nader Report* (Washington, D.C.: 1980), page 107.

THE HUMANITARIAN

"It's just too bad we can't have an epidemic of botulism."

■ Govenor Reagan was wishing often-fatal food poisoning upon poor Californians to whom he was releasing — very much against his will — $2 million worth of surplus foodstuffs. He had yielded to pressure from a group of radical fanatics calling themselves the Symbionese Liberation Army, and not, it may be emphasized, to pressure from the hungry.

After the statement was publicized, a Reagan spokesman nibbled at the accuracy of the quote in word but not in spirit. The governor's words, he said, had been closer to, "Sometimes you wonder whether there shouldn't be an outbreak of botulism."

Reagan himself wrote to a congressman that his remark "was uttered in a private gathering and certainly not as a joke. ... It was one of those exaggerations that we all at times utter to express frustration, and we do so with confidence that no one takes us literally."

The New York Times reported the statement on 8 March 1974. Ronnie Dugger reported the variant and the letter to the legislator in his book *On Reagan: The Man & His Presidency.*

THE TITHER

"I also happen to be someone who believes in tithing — the giving of a tenth. But I have for a number of years done some of that giving in ways that are not tax deductible with regard to individuals that are being helped."[1]

■ Response to a question by Washington Post columnist Mary McGrory: "Are you planning to increase your own contributions to private charity to set an example to the rich people of this country to do more for the poor?"

The day following the exchange, White House spokesman Larry Speakes tattered the tither by admitting that Reagan's *current* rate of contributing didn't come close to a tenth. Moreover, McGrory wrote later, the Reagans' income-tax return had revealed, in the President's words, what "seemed to be a small percentage of deductions for worthwhile causes."[2]

---

1. Press conference, 19 January 1982.
2. Mary McGrory, 22 June 1986.

THE MORALIST

"There can be no moral justification for the progressive income tax."

Syndicated radio broadcast, 22 December 1978.

THE TAX SLASHER

"If I can quote you from your own ad," said ABC News Correspondent John Laurence, *"you're saying on camera, 'I didn't always agree with President Kennedy, but when his 30 percent Federal tax cut became law, the economy did so well that every group in the country came out ahead. If I become President, we're going to try that again.' Do you remember saying those words?"*

"I don't remember saying that because I honestly don't know what the rate of tax cut was."

"Well, perhaps someone else wrote them for you."

"I'm sure, but I don't even remember reading that."

ABC News' television program "Issues and Answers," 16 March 1980.

THE REGULATOR

"I've been told that something like 42 trillion rate decisions were given by the ICC [Interstate Commerce Commission] in its 85-year history and that they are not even indexed."

■   The 42,000,000,000,000 decisions break down to 56,368,000 an hour — 24 hours a day, seven days a week, 52 weeks a year, allowing for Leap Years. Or more than 900,000 a minute. Try it on your calculator. Incidentally, the ICC had been in existence for 89 years.

"Government Regualtion: What Kind of Reform?", a televised round table discussion held 11 September 1975, and sponsored by the American Enterprise Institute for Public Policy Research and the Hoover Institution on War, Revolution and Peace.

THE MEDICINES MAN

'I think something more than 40,000 tuberculars alone have died in this country who conceivably could have been saved by a drug that has been used widely in the last few years throughout Europe."[1]

■ Reagan was arguing that U.S. drug regulation, because strict, needlessly killed Americans by depriving them of wonder drugs available in other countries. His example was rifampin, invented in Italy and put on sale there in 1968. Two U.S. firms applied to sell it at the end of 1970. The Food and Drug Administration granted approval a swift five months later, five years *before* Reagan spoke.

Government statistics show that in the few months in which the FDA had the application, U.S. TB deaths from *all* causes, lack of early diagnosis probably being the most important, was about 1,750. The advent of rifampin hardly caused TB death to plummet. Rather, they continued an uneven decline; and the U.S. total *from all causes* for the nine years through 1978 was nearly one-third fewer than he blamed on a single cause.[2]

---

1. American Enterprise Institute TV program, 11 September 1975.
2. The refutation is from the Washington Post, 20 December 1980.

THE OBSTETRICIAN

"I think the fact that children have been prematurely born even down to the three-month stage and have lived to, the record shows, to grow up and be normal human beings, that ought to be enough for all of us."[1]

■   "At three months most women aren't even in maternity clothes," Washington Post columnist Judy Mann wrote. "Even at the end of three months, fetuses are only $3\frac{1}{2}$ inches long, according to the American College of Obstetricians and Gynecologists ...

"Morton Blackwell, special assistant to the President for religious groups, called Jack C. Willke, president of the National Right to Life Committee, trying to find out if any three-month fetuses had ever survived," Mann wrote, "Willke said no."[2]

---

1. Statement made 14 September 1982, to a meeting of religion editors and promptly discredited by the Associated Press.
2. 17 September 1982.

THE ENERGY CONSERVER

"Fuel used on Amtrak [trains] is 48 passenger miles per gallon, exactly the same as the average automobile."

■ This Reagan effort to show trains to be no more energy-efficient than cars was a stigmata of his campaign to kill Amtrak, the federally-subsidized passenger train network. The effort was, however, derailed by a Department of Transportation finding: a 14-car train travelling at 80 miles per hour gets 400 passenger-miles to the gallon — nearly *ten times* the 42.6 passenger-miles per gallon achieved by a fuel-efficient 1985 car carrying an average of 2.2 occupants.

Syndicated radio commentary broadcast on various days in July 1979 and edited by Edward Flattan, Chicago Tribune, 10 May 1980.

THE GEIGER COUNTER

"Smoke from a coal-burning plant releases more radioactivity into the air than comes from a nuclear plant."

Talk at Stevens High School, Claremont, New Hampshire, 18 February 1980.

THE GEOLOGIST

"One survey by two men, Mr. Mull and Mr. Koseloff, of the U.S. Geological Survey, in 1976, done for the Fish and Wildlife Service, says that Alaska has a potential [petroleum reserve] that is greater than the known reserves of Saudi Arabia."[1]

■ Charles Mull said the survey "made no estimates" of the Alaskan oil potential. His co-author, whose name is *Kososki*, said the survey "never made a comparison" between petroleum reserves in Alaska and Saudi Arabia. At the time, Alaska had 9 billion barrels or proven petroleum reserves and Saudi Arabia 165 billion barrels, or more than 18 times as many. Alaska's *potential* was less than one-third of Saudi Arabia's *proven* total.[2]

1. CBS News, 3 April 1980
2. Washington Post, 31 March 1980.

THE CONSERVATIONIST

"A tree is a tree. How many more do you need
to look at?"

■   A statement made in opposition to expansion
     of California's Redwoods Park.

---

12 March 1966.

THE NATURE LOVER I

"The American Petroleum Institute filed suit against the Environmental Protection Agency [and] charged that the agency was suppressing a scientific study for fear it might be misinterpreted. ... The suppressed study reveals that 80% of air pollution comes not from chimneys and auto exhaust pipes, but from plants and trees."[1]

■ No support whatever for this leafy claim is provided by the listing of "National Air Pollutant Emissions, by Pollutant and Emissions Source" in the authoritative *Statistical Abstract of the United States*.

 Waggish opponents hung posters on trees saying: 'Cut me down before I kill again.'[2]

---

1. Excerpted by Ronnie Dugger in his book, *On Reagan*, from a radio talk broadcast in January and February 1979.
2. The Observer, 5th January 1986.

THE NATURE LOVER II

"I know Teddy Kennedy had fun at the Democratic convention when he said that I had said that trees and vegetation cause 80% of the air pollution in this country. Well, now he was a little wrong about what I said. First of all, I didn't say 80%, I said 92%, 93%, pardon me. And I didn't say air pollution. I said oxides of nitrogen. And I am right. Growing and decaying vegetation in this land are responsible for 93% of the oxides of nitrogen."

■ "Reagan apparently had confused nitrous oxide, which growing plants emit, with nitrogen dioxide, which is emitted by smokestacks," Lou Cannon wrote in *Reagan*. Besides, Kennedy had quoted him correctly [see The Nature-Lover I].

Campaign speech in Steubeuville, Ohio, 7 October 1980.

THE NATURE LOVER III

"I have flown twice over Mount St. Helens out on our West Coast. I'm not a scientist and I don't know the figures, but I just have a suspicion that that one little mountain has probably released more sulphur dioxide into the atmosphere of the world than has been released in the last ten years of automobile driving or things of that kind that people are so concerned about."[1]

■　Reagan "wasn't even close to being right in his guess about the volcanic Mount St. Helens, which at its peak activity was producing 2,000 tons of sulphur dioxide a day, compared to 81,000 tons of sulphur dioxide produced each day by automobiles."[2]

---

1. Campaign speech in Steubenville, Ohio, 7 October 1980.
2. Washington Post reporter Lou Cannon, in his book *Reagan*.

THE INTELLECTUAL

"The State of California has no business
subsidizing intellectual curiosity."

■   Governor Reagan's outraged reaction to
student unrest during his first term in
California.

Time, 31 March 1980.

THE REPUBLICAN LEADER

"Now, the simple truth is those Democrats who are here are probably here because like millions I've met across the country, they have found they can no longer follow the leadership of the Republican Party, which has taken them down a course that leads to disaster."

Talk at a political campaign rally for Republican Senate candidate Jim Santini, Las Vegas, Nevada, on the eve of the election of 4 November 1986. "Mr. Reagan apparently mis-spoke," the New York Times said. Santini lost.

THE NAVIGATOR

"I can't tell until somebody tells me. . . . I never know where I'm going."

■ Reagan's response when asked if he'd be visiting the Vietnam War Memorial on Veterans Day.

Exchange with reporters, 9 November 1982.

THE COMMANDER-IN-CHIEF I

"Anything we do is in our national security interest."

■ The President had been asked, "Would you like to talk about the helicopters to Bolivia [for use against cocaine growers]? Is that in our national security interest?"

Informal exchange with reporters at the White House preceding the President's meeting with Prime Minister Mohammad Khan Junejo of Pakistan, 16 July 1986.

THE COMMANDER-IN-CHIEF II

"We did not condone, and do not condone, the shipment of arms from other countries. ... we, as I say, have had nothing to do with other countries or their shipment of arms ..."

■ Reagan's responses on being asked how secret U.S. and Israeli arms shipments to Iran could not have violated the National Security Act.

A reporter returned to the subject:

"We've been told by the chief of staff, Donald Regan, that ... this government condoned an Israeli shipment in September of 1985, ..."

Reagan: "... I never heard Mr. Regan say that, and I'll ask him about that because we believe in the [Iran arms] embargo ..."

A written "Statement by the President," issued 25 minutes after the press conference, said:

"There was a third country involved in our secret project with Iran."

■ Israel confirmed it was that country eight days later.

White House press conference, 18 November 1986.

THE COMMANDER-IN-CHIEF III

*Reporter, asking about the Iran arms affair: "...
what would be wrong in saying that a mistake
was made on a very high-risk gamble so that you
can get on with the next two years?"*

"Because I don't think a mistake was made."

Seven days later, an interviewer raised the same
question.

"I do not think it was a mistake."

Ten days after that:

"... it's obvious that the execution of these
policies was flawed and mistakes were made."

Press conference, 19 November 1986; interview was Hugh
Sidey, Time, 26 November 1986; weekly address, 6 December
1986.

THE COMMANDER-IN-CHIEF IV

"And I really mean, when all these indications that maybe I know more than I'm talking about — I'm trying to find out, too, what happened."

■ Reagan said this after Adm. John M. Poindexter, his former National Security Adviser, and Lt. Col. Oliver L. North, Poindexter's key aide, had invoked the Fifth Amendment protection against self-incrimination. The President had just cited his endorsement of various investigations and other actions intended to establish all of the facts about the Iran arms deal.

Talk to a group of small-business leaders, 23 December 1986

THE OBSERVER

Reporter: "Do you ever look down from the upper floors of the White House, across to Lafayette Park where a soup kitchen is set up for the city's hungry and homeless? Have you ever noticed these people?"

"I didn't know that was going on, but I'll make a point [of looking] now that you've told me. You see, the living quarters are on the opposite side of the White House so there is very little occasion to go and look out. The one room I do use [on the north side] is the exercise room."

■ Now, if you look rightward to the facing page, you will share the President's vision — you will see what he saw in one northward look from the exercise room.

People Magazine, 1982-1983 combined year-end issue dated 27 December 1982 and 3 January 1983.

THE PRESIDENT
FOR ALL SEASONS

"In December, when I looked north from the White House, I would see the huge menorah celebrating the Passover season in Lafayette Park."

■ It was the winter Hanukkah season, not the spring Passover season, when the President gazed northward from what he termed "a special vantage point from which to judge" indications that the importance of religious faith to Americans has grown stronger.

Remarks to the National Religious Broadcasters, 4 February 1985.

THE BULB SNATCHER

"Now, I know this from personal experience with one of the Generals, General Electric. At one stage, some years ago, GE could produce light bulbs for half the price at which it was selling them ... but GE already had such a large share of the market that it didn't dare reduce the price as low as it could have, because if it had captured any more of the market, it would have been in trouble with the government."[1]

■ One may be tempted to believe Reagan was authoritative, on the assumption that his several years in the employ of GE — as a speechmaker — gave him access to inside information. But GE itself cast a dim light on his claim, saying it was "wholly unable to identify any single system ... which had the effect of cutting in half the cost of manufacturing our household type lamp bulbs."[2]

---

1. American Enterprise Institute television program, 11 September 1975.
2. GE turned off his lamp in a letter to the Public Citizen Corporate. Accountability Research Group as reprinted in the Sacramento Bee on 3 June 1976.

THE FACT CHECKER

'Governor," said CBS News Correspondent Bill Plante, "generally speaking, are you satisfied that you have done a thorough enough job of checking your basic material?'

"Yes I do. I've been on the mashed potato circuit for a great many years, probably a quarter of a century. And I learned very early that you should check them. I didn't at first, I guess, like any other speaker. I'd see something and think, hey, that's great, and use it. And I just learned from being rebutted a couple of times that I'd better be sure of my facts."

CBS Evening News with Walter Cronkite, 3 April 1980.

THE WINNER

"Mr. President, Lou Cannon, a reporter widely known for not only having covered you a long time, but also for his efforts to be fair to you before and since you've been in the White House, Lou Cannon recently made, and I quote, 'More disquieting than Reagan's performance or prospects on specific issues is a growing suspicion that the President has only a passing acquaintance with some of the most important decisions of his Administration.' End of quotation. I think he meant specifically on foreign policy. Is that fair criticism?"

'No. And it's absolutely false, and I was quite shocked when I read it. This whole effort that goes clear back into the campaign, and including the last press conference, to have me constantly out mis-stating facts, I — someday we can sit down and I would like to match my accuracy with that of the media and I think I'd come out on top."

"A Conversation with the President," Dan Rather, CBS Television Network, 27 January 1982.